W9-BMN-213

50 words about
Plants

David and Patricia Armentrout

Rourke

Publishing LLC
Vero Beach, Florida 32964

www.rourkepublishing.com

PHOTO CREDITS: © Brand X Pictures Cover, page 21 top; © James P. Rowan page 23 top; © Corel pages 5 bottom, 17; © Louisiana Department of Tourism page 15 bottom; © Painet, Inc. pages 6 bottom, 13 bottom; © Armentrout pages 7 bottom, 8 top, 10 top, 12 bottom, 14 bottom, 18 top, 20 bottom; © Canola Council of Canada pages 10 bottom, 19 top, 26 top; © PhotoDisc all other photos

Editor: Frank Sloan

Cover and page design by Nicola Stratford

Library of Congress Cataloging-in-Publication Data

Armentrout, David, 1962-
  Plants / David and Patricia Armentrout.
      p. cm. — (50 words about)
Summary: Provides simple definitions for fifty words related to plants
along with sample sentences using each word.
   ISBN 1-58952-345-8 (Hardcover)
   1. Plants—Juvenile literature. [1. Plants—Dictionaries.] I.
Armentrout, Patricia, 1960- II. Title.

   QK49 .A74 2002
   580—dc21

                                                                                    2002002375

Printed in the USA

CG/CG

plant (PLANT)

A living thing that uses sunlight to make its own food.

algae

Small plants without roots or stems that grow in water.

Algae cover the surface of the water in this southern swamp.

bark

The hard covering on a tree trunk.

A tree's tough bark protects it from hazards like this bear's claws.

berry

A small, colorful fruit found on bushes and trees.

Some berries are good to eat, but others are very poisonous.

blade

A single piece of grass.

One blade of grass may not look like much, but a field of grass provides a home to many kinds of animals.

blossom

A flower on a plant or fruit tree.

The blossom is often the most colorful part of a plant.

botany

The scientific study of plants.

There is no place better to study botany than a lush green meadow.

bud

A blossom that has not yet opened.

The buds on this plant will soon sprout into beautiful blossoms.

bulb

The onion-shaped part of some plants that grow underground.

A bulb planted in the fall will grow into a new plant in the spring.

burr

A prickly seed case, or pod, that sticks to clothes and animal fur.

A hike in an overgrown field can leave you covered in burrs.

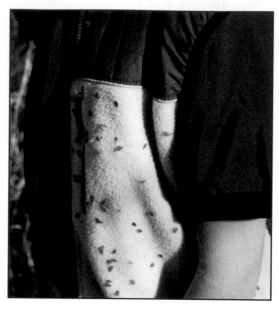

bush

A small tree that has lots of branches and leaves.

Just like some trees, a bush can lose its leaves in the fall.

cactus

A plant with sharp spikes instead of leaves that grows in hot, dry areas.

The cactus plant is most common in desert areas.

chlorophyll

The substance that gives green plants color.

Chlorophyll absorbs energy from the Sun.

conifer

An evergreen tree that grows cones.

Pine cones grow on conifer trees.

crop

A plant grown in large amounts.

Some farmers make money by growing and selling a crop.

deciduous

Trees that shed their leaves every year.

Before falling off, leaves on deciduous trees may turn shades of yellow, orange, and red.

evergreen

A plant that keeps green leaves year round.

An evergreen forest is always green.

fern

A plant with feathery leaves and no flowers.

A fern is a popular houseplant.

fertilize

To add nutrients to soil to help plants grow better.

Grass will grow stronger and greener if you fertilize it.

flower

The colorful part of a plant that makes seeds.

The giant flower on this sunflower plant grows edible seeds.

fruit

The fleshy part of a plant that contains one or more seeds.

Fruit is good for the body.

fungus

A plant that has no leaves, roots, or flowers.

A mushroom plant is a kind of fungus.

garden

A piece of land used by people to grow plants.

Planting a garden can be fun, but dirty, work.

grow

To get bigger in size.

A giant Redwood tree can grow big enough to drive a car through it.

harvest

To gather crops that are ripe.

Big machines make harvest time much easier.

leaf

The thin, flat part of a plant that grows from a stem.

This leaf has turned from green to red and will soon fall from the tree.

limb

A branch of a tree.

This raccoon really knows what it means to go out on a limb.

moss

A small furry green plant that grows on rocks and trees.

Moss grows best in moist, shaded areas.

needle

A thin, pointed leaf on pine and fir trees.

The needle works to make food for the tree.

nursery

A place that grows and sells plants.

It's easy to find beautiful plants at a nursery.

nut

A fruit or seed that has a hard shell called a hull.

It takes some work to get to it, but a Brazil nut is good eating.

pesticide

A chemical used to kill pests.

A crop duster is used to spray pesticide on a crop.

pests

Insects that destroy plants.

Bagworms are sometimes called pests because they feed on the leaves of trees.

petal

A colorful part of a flower.

The orchid is a popular flower because of its colorful petals.

photosynthesis

A process where plants use the Sun's energy to make their own food.

Without sunlight, grass will die because it is unable to use photosynthesis to make food.

pollen

Small yellow grains made in the flower of plants.

Bees carry pollen from one plant to the next as they search for food.

root

The part of a plant that grows underground.

Soil has broken away and uncovered the roots of these trees.

seed

The part of a plant that can grow new plants.

A single dandelion flower produces many seeds.

seedling

A young plant that has grown from a seed.

A seedling such as this will someday grow into a huge tree.

soil

The dirt that plants grow in.

Soil contains nutrients that help a plant grow.

stamen

The part of a flower that makes pollen.

The stamen are surrounded by white petals.

stem

The parts of a plant that leaves and flowers grow from.

A tree frog rests on the stem of this plant.

stigma

stigma

The part of the flower that receives pollen.

The stigma can usually be found in the center of the flower.

sunlight

Light from the Sun that gives plants energy and warms the Earth.

Life on earth would not be possible without sunlight.

thorn

A sharp point on a stem or branch.

A cactus thorn protects it from hungry animals.

till

To prepare land for growing crops.

Farmers till their fields before planting crops.

tree

A big, tall plant with a thick trunk, branches, and leaves.

A flowering tree blooms in early spring.

vegetable

A plant that is grown for food.

Corn is one of the most common vegetable crops grown in the United States.

vine

A plant with a long, climbing stem.

Vines might be fun, but they can damage trees over time.

water

A clear liquid needed by all living things.

A duck uses webbed feet to swim silently through the water.

weed

A plant that grows where it is not wanted.

People spend a lot of time getting rid of the weeds in their gardens.

Pronunciation Key

algae (AL gee)
bark (BARK)
berry (BAIR ee)
blade (BLAYD)
blossom (BLOSS uhm)
botany (BOT uh nee)
bud (BUHD)
bulb (BUHLB)
bur (BUR)
bush (BUSH)
cactus (KAK tuss)
chlorophyll (KLOR uh fill)
conifer (KON uh fur)
crop (KROP)
deciduous (di SIJ yoo uhss)
evergreen (EV er green)
fern (FURN)
fertilize (FUR tuh lize)
flower (FLOU ur)
fruit (FROOT)
fungus (FUHN guhss)
garden (GARD uhn)
grow (GROH)
harvest (HAR vist)
leaf (LEEF)
limb (LIM)

moss (MAWSS)
needle (NEE duhl)
nursery (NUR sur ee)
nut (NUHT)
pesticide (PESS tuh side)
pests (PESTS)
petal (PET uhl)
photosynthesis
   (foe toe SIN thuh siss)
pollen (POL uhn)
root (ROOT)
seed (SEED)
seedling (SEED ling)
soil (SOYL)
stamen (STAY muhn)
stem (STEM)
stigma (STIG muh)
sunlight (SUHN lite)
thorn (THORN)
till (TIL)
tree (TREE)
vegetable (VEJ tuh buhl)
vine (VINE)
water (WA tur)
weed (WEED)

Did you know...

...plants first appeared on Earth about 500 million years ago? Today, scientists have named more than 260,000 kinds of plants.

Did you know...

...plants provide people and animals with food, shelter, medicine, and even the air we breathe?

Did you know...

...some plants are poisonous? Some mushroom plants can be eaten, while others can make you very sick.

Did you know...

...bamboo is one of the fastest growing plants? Some types of bamboo grow 24 inches (60.9 centimeters) in a single day.

Did you know...

...redwood trees are among the tallest and largest living things on Earth? Some giant sequoia redwoods weigh over 2,500 tons! (2,268 metric tons)

Did you know...

...some plants are carnivorous, or meat-eaters? Some carnivorous plants eat insects, while others capture small frogs and birds!

Index

Further Reading

The Visual Dictionary of Plants. Dorling Kindersley, 1992

Websites to Visit

www.enchantedlearning.com

www.pbs.org

www.nationalgeographic.org

About the Authors

David and Patricia Armentrout specialize in nonfiction writing. They have had several books published for primary school reading. They reside in Cincinnati, Ohio, with their two children.

32